49

nts

J   580503
534   9.95
Woo
Wood
Physics for kids, 49 easy
    experiments with acoustics

DATE DUE			
MRO 5 '88			

PHYSICS
FOR KIDS

49 Easy Experiments
with Acoustics

Robert W. Wood

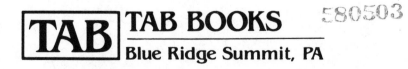

TAB | **TAB BOOKS**
Blue Ridge Summit, PA

FIRST EDITION
SECOND PRINTING

Library of Congress Cataloging-in-Publication Data

Wood, Robert W., 1933 –
   Physics for kids : 49 easy experiments with acoustics / by Robert
W. Wood.
     p.   cm.
   Includes index.
   Summary: Examines the principles of sound through simple
experiments.
   ISBN 0-8306-7392-X   ISBN 0-8306-3392-8 (pbk.)
   1. Sound—Experiments—Juvenile literature.   2. Sound-waves-
-Experiments—Juvenile literature. [1. Sound—Experiments.
2. Experiments.] I. Title.
QC225.5.W66 1990
534—dc20   90-40038
                                 CIP
                                 AC

TAB Books offers software for sale. For information and a catalog, please contact TAB Software Department, Blue Ridge Summit, PA 17294-0850.

Acquisitions Editor: Kimberly Tabor
Book Editor: Lori Flaherty
Director of Production: Katherine G. Brown   HT3

Contents

Introduction

Physics is a term that comes from a Greek word that means nature. It is the science that studies the "how" and "why" of the natural world around us. Physics explains what makes thunder, how a satellite stays up, and why stars twinkle.

The subjects in this exciting field often overlap, but they can be divided into several basic groups: mechanics, heat, light, electricity and magnetism, and sound. This book is about the fascinating field of acoustics, or sound.

Sound is all around us: the wind, a dog barking, the voices of people on the street, and the singing of birds. A world without sound would be unpleasant. But where does sound come from? When something vibrates, it vibrates the air around it. When the vibrating object moves in one direction, it pushes the air, causing it to compress. Then, when the object moves back, air rushes in to fill the space, causing the air to expand. The compressing and expanding air near the object also makes the air at a distance compress and expand. This means that the vibration travels through the air much like ripples from a rock that is dropped in a pool. The vibrations are called sound waves. Sound must have something to travel through. It cannot travel in a vacuum. The speed it travels depends on how dense the substance is. For example, sound travels about 1,100 feet per second through the air, about 4,700 feet per second through water, and about 1,600 feet per second through steel.

Scientists study sound and the affects it has on people. Hospitals and libraries must be designed so that they will have quiet areas, while auditoriums are built to carry sound to people in the audience. Sound is an exciting and important branch of physics, and the experiments in this book present the basics for understanding how sound works and some of the ways man influences sound.

Conduct all of the experiments in this book with safety in mind. Be careful; some experiments require an adult to help you. If you are just the least bit unsure about anything, ask a parent or teacher for help or advice before you begin. Be sure to read the Symbols Used in This Book section that follows. These symbols will alert you to any safety precautions you should take and whether an adult should help you.

Symbols Used in This Book

All of the experiments in this book can be done safely, but it is recommended that a parent or teacher supervise young children and instruct them on any potential hazards.

The following symbols are used throughout the book for you to use as a guide to what children might be able to do independently, and what they *should not do* without adult supervision. Keep in mind that some children might not be mature enough to do any of the experiments without adult help, and that these symbols should be used as a guide only and do not replace the good judgment of parents or teachers.

 Flame is used in this project and adult supervision is required. Do not wear loose clothing. Tie hair back. When handling candles, wear protective gloves—hot wax can burn. Never leave a flame unattended. Extinguish flame properly. Protect surfaces beneath burning candles.

 The use of the stove, boiling water, or other hot materials are used in this project and adult supervision is required. Keep other small children away from boiling water and burners.

 Protective gloves that are flame retardant and heat resistant should be worn. Handling hot objects and hot wax can burn hands. Protect surfaces beneath hot materials—do not set pots of boiling water or very hot objects directly on table-tops or counters. Use towels or heat pads.

 Materials or tools used in this experiment could be dangerous in young hands. Adult supervision is recommended. Be sure to keep tools and materials out of reach of young children after use.

 Scissors are used in this project. Young children should be supervised carefully and older children instructed to exercise caution.

Electricity is used in this experiment. Young children should be supervised and older children cautioned about the hazards of electricity.

 Protective safety goggles should be worn to protect against shattering glass, flying debris, and other hazards that could damage the eyes.

PART I

49 EASY EXPERIMENTS
IN ACOUSTICS

Experiment 1

Discovering What Sound Is

Materials

- [ ] table
- [ ] hacksaw blade
- [ ] yardstick
- [ ] rubber bands of different thicknesses
- [ ] small wooden or cardboard box

Place the hacksaw blade about halfway over the edge of the table. Press down firmly and thump the extended end with your finger (Fig. 1-1). Repeat the steps, gradually sticking more of the blade over the edge. Try the same experiment with the yardstick and compare the different sounds (Fig. 1-2). Now stretch different sized rubber bands

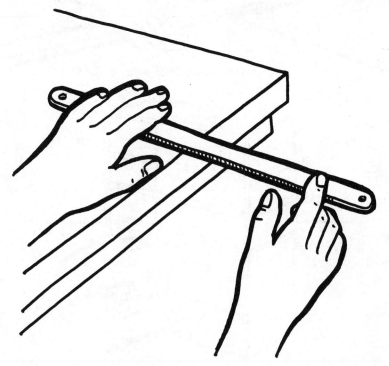

Fig. 1-1. Extend the hacksaw blade over the edge of the table.

Fig. 1-2. *The vibrating yardstick produces the sound.*

Fig. 1-3. *Vibrating rubber bands produce sound.*

over the box. Pluck each one separately (Fig. 1-3). Try stretching some tighter and notice the change in the sound.

The sounds produced by the saw blade and the rubber bands were caused by vibrations. How fast something vibrates determines the pitch of the sound. This is the frequency. It is the number of times an object, or the sound waves it produces, vibrate in a second. The higher the frequency, the higher the pitch.

Experiment 2

Materials

- [ ] watch with a second hand
- [ ] thunderstorm

Measuring the Distance to a Thunderstorm

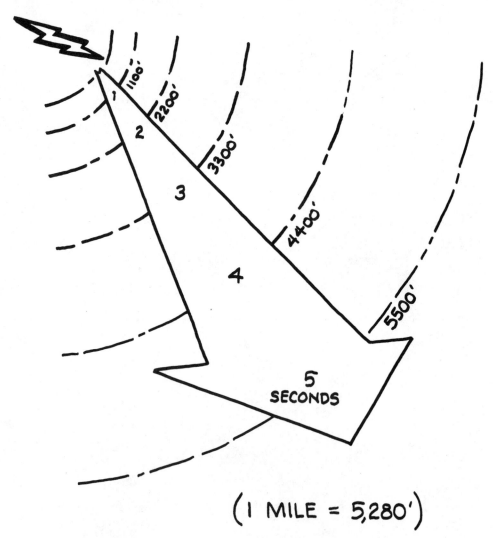

$$(1 \text{ MILE} = 5{,}280')$$

Fig. 2-1. *Sound travels at about 1,100 feet per second through the air.*

Watch for a flash of lightning. The instant you see the flash, start counting the seconds until you hear the thunder. The length of time it takes the sound of the lightning to reach us tells us how far we are from the lightning. This is because sound travels through the air at about 1,100 feet per second. Multiply the speed times the number of seconds. If it takes five seconds for the thunder to reach us, the distance will be about 5,500 feet, or a little over a mile (Fig. 2-1). If a watch is not handy, simply count "thousand one, thousand two, thousand three, etc.," to represent each second.

Experiment 3

Sound Waves from a Rubber Band

Materials

- ☐ dry cereal such as puffed rice (about 10 pieces)
- ☐ sewing thread
- ☐ coat hanger
- ☐ rubber band stretched between the ends of a curved stick
- ☐ scissors

Cut several lengths of thread, one for each piece of cereal kernel (Fig. 3-1). Tie one end around a piece of cereal and the other end to the bottom of the coat hanger. Repeat the steps until you have suspended about 10 kernels an equal distance across the coat hanger (Fig. 3-2).

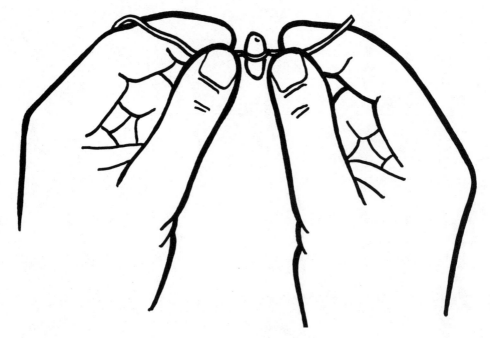

Fig. 3-1. *Tie the thread to the puffed rice.*

Hook the hanger over an open door way or over the back of a chair. Hold the rubber band near the center, but not touching, the suspended pieces of cereal kernels. Pluck the rubber band. The kernels will move back and forth (Fig. 3-3).

The kernels closest to the rubber band will move the most but none will move very much. The vibration of the rubber band caused the movement, which made the air around it move. This air bumped into the air next to it and caused it to move. This action continued outward, like waves, until the waves became weak and faded away.

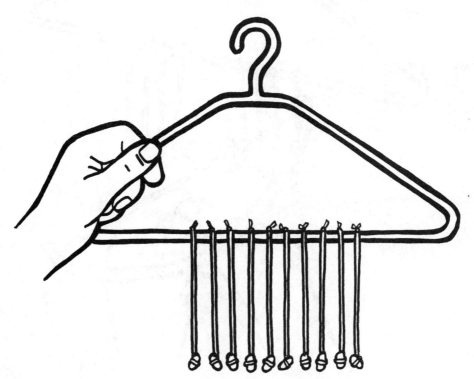

Fig. 3-2. *Suspend the rice from a coat hanger.*

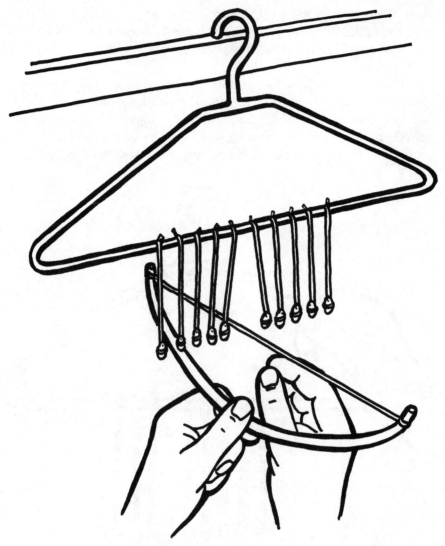

Fig. 3-3. *Pluck the rubber band and watch the puffed rice.*

Experiment 4

How Sound Waves are Reflected

Materials

☐ small rope, about 20 feet long (clothesline rope)
☐ tree

Tie one end of the rope around the tree, about waist high (Fig. 4-1). Stretch out the rope, but leave a little slack in it. Grasp the free end of the rope in your hand and jerk it downward suddenly. A hump

Fig. 4-1. Tie the rope to the tree.

will form in the rope and quickly travel away from you (Fig. 4-2). The hump will travel the length of the rope until it reaches the tree. There, the knot keeps the hump from rising and it is whipped downward. At that point, the hump is upside down and turns into a hollow, where it quickly travels back down the rope to your hand (Fig. 4-3). The hump that you made travel along the rope was reflected back when it hit the knot at the tree. This is the same way ripples on a pond are reflected from the banks and sound waves are reflected from the side of a building or the walls in a theater.

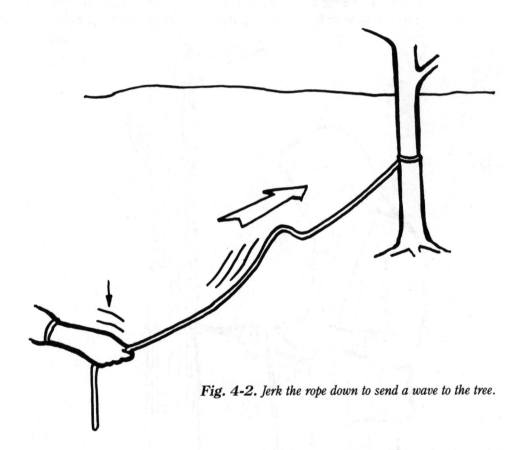

Fig. 4-2. *Jerk the rope down to send a wave to the tree.*

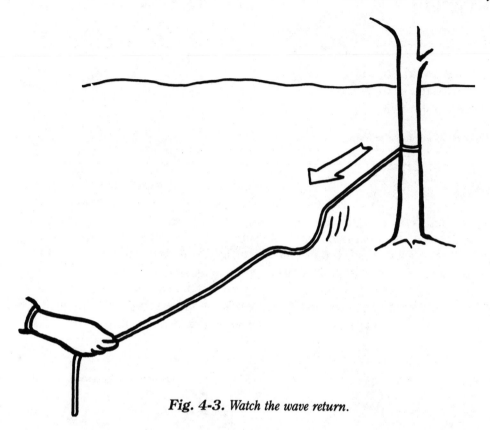

Fig. 4-3. *Watch the wave return.*

Experiment 5

Sound Wave Patterns in a Room

Place the pan on a level surface and fill it with about an inch of water (Fig. 5-1). Let the water stand until the surface is smooth and flat. Now, using the medicine dropper, drop a single drop of water into the pan near one end (Fig. 5-2). Notice how the ripples spread out in all directions. When they strike the sides of the pan, they are reflected back in a new direction. This happens again and again until the ripples fade away. Try dropping the drop of water near one of the corners. Notice that the pattern of the ripples is the same except they travel at a different angle and are reflected at different angles from the sides (Fig. 5-3).

Fig. 5-1. *Pour water in the pan.*

If you could see sound waves, and were able to look down into a room shaped like the pan, you could see sound waves behaving like the ripples. The point where the drop hit the water could be where someone was speaking.

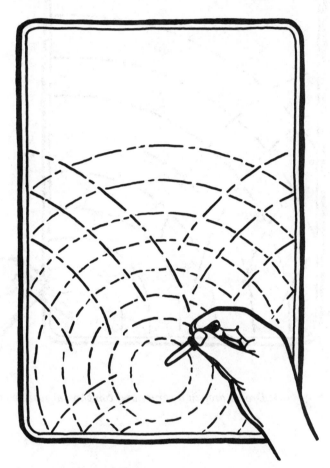

Fig. 5-2. *Drop one drop in the center and notice the pattern of the waves.*

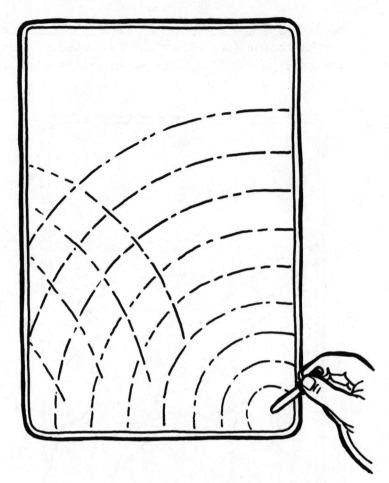

Fig. 5-3. *Drop a drop in a corner and compare the wave patterns.*

Experiment 6

Reflecting Sound Waves

Materials

- ☐ **2 people**
- ☐ **2 cardboard tubes from paper towels**
- ☐ **ticking watch or clock**
- ☐ **table**

Hold the watch or clock near the end of one of the tubes (Fig. 6-1). Place the tube at an angle with the open end near the top of the table. Ask someone to hold the other tube at an opposite angle and listen at the end of their tube (Fig. 6-2). They should plug their other ear with their finger to reduce outside sounds, so that they can hear the ticking

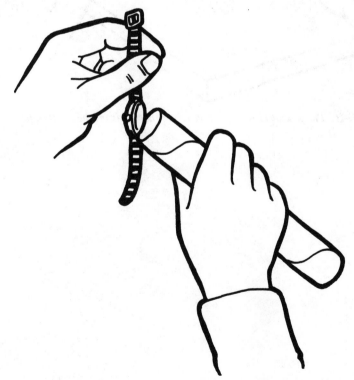

Fig. 6-1. Place the watch at one end of the tube.

of the watch through the tube. When the positions of the tubes are just right, the ticking can be heard coming out of the end of the second tube.

The sound waves travel down the first tube and are reflected off the surface of the table into the second tube. They then travel up the second tube and are heard at the opening. Sound waves can be reflected much like rays of light are reflected by a mirror.

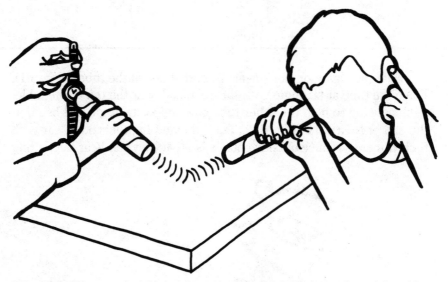

Fig. 6-2. *The sound of the watch can be reflected from the surface of the table.*

Experiment 7

The Vibrating Speakers

Materials

- ☐ speaker from radio or stereo
- ☐ music from speaker
- ☐ sheet of paper
- ☐ transparent tape

Turn the sound level down low on the radio or stereo and tape the paper to the front of the speaker (Fig. 7-1). Notice how the paper vibrates. Gradually increase the sound level and watch the paper vibrate (Fig. 7-2). Place your hand on the paper and feel the vibrations. These are waves of air that produce waves of sound. The wires connected to the speaker are carrying electrical signals that vary with the sounds of the music. The electrical signals causes a coil inside a magnet at the back of the speaker's cone to vibrate. This vibrates the cone producing waves of air (Fig. 7-3). When these waves reach your ear, they are sensed by delicate nerves connected to the eardrum and converted into sound.

Fig. 7-1. *Tape the paper to the front of the speaker.*

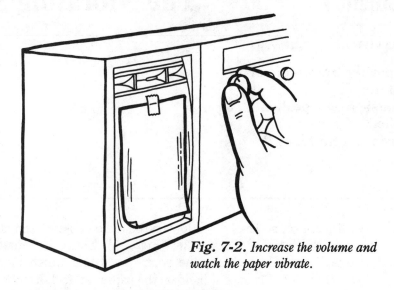

Fig. 7-2. *Increase the volume and watch the paper vibrate.*

SPEAKER
(SIDE VIEW)

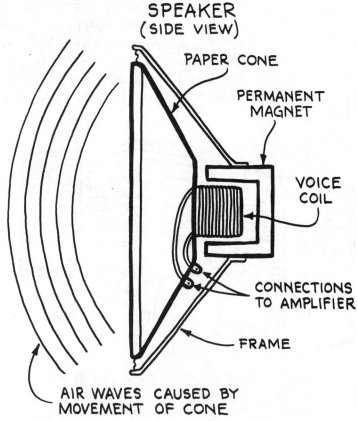

PAPER CONE

PERMANENT MAGNET

VOICE COIL

CONNECTIONS TO AMPLIFIER

FRAME

AIR WAVES CAUSED BY MOVEMENT OF CONE

Fig. 7-3. *Electrical signals makes the cone vibrate, reproducing the sound.*

Experiment 8

Materials

- [ ] candle and adults
- [ ] empty round box (salt box or oat cereal box with lid)
- [ ] scissors
- [ ] transparent tape

How to Make an Air Shock Wave

Remove the metal spout from the salt box (Fig. 8-1). If an oat box is used, cut a hole in the center of the bottom about the size of a dime and tape the lid in place on the top. Have an adult place a lighted candle on a table and aim the box at the flame. Have the end with the hole pointing at the candle. Thump the other end of the box with your finger (Fig. 8-2). You might have to try two or three times to adjust your aim but you should be able to blow out the flame from several feet away (Fig. 8-3).

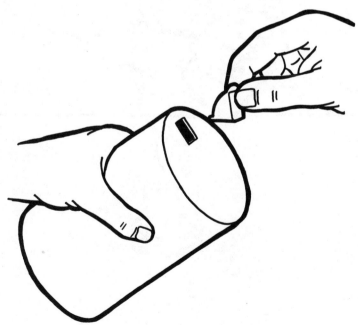

Fig. 8-1. Remove the spout from the empty salt box.

The thump on the end of the box sent a shock wave out of the hole. This wave was strong enough to put out the candle but was too low of a frequency to be heard as sound. The human ear can detect sound vibrations of about 20 to 20,000 per second.

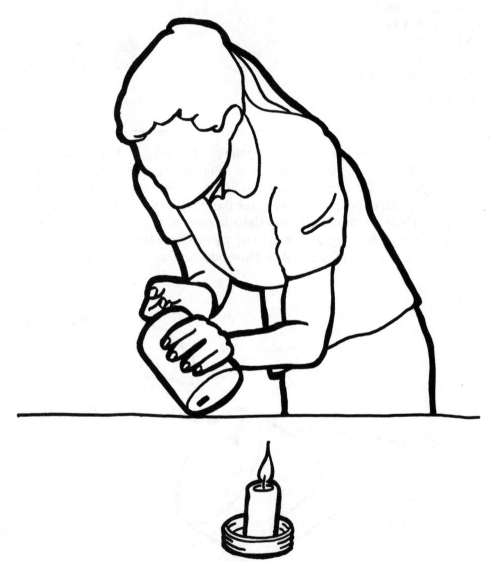

Fig. 8-2. Thump the end of the box.

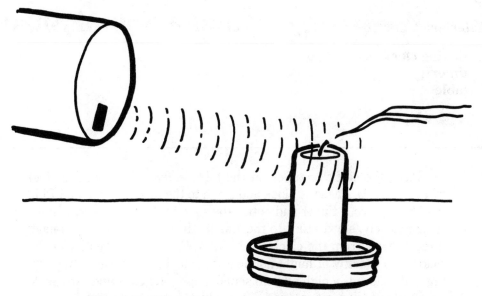

Fig. 8-3. *The flame can be put out from several feet away.*

Experiment 9

Materials

☐ **ticking clock or kitchen timer**
☐ **table**

High-Pitched Sounds and a Sound Shadow

Place the clock or timer on the table and stand about four feet away (Fig. 9-1). Face the clock and listen to the ticking (Fig. 9-2). Plug one ear with your finger and notice the sound (Fig. 9-3). Now, still listening closely, slowly turn to the side so that your open ear is facing directly away from the clock as shown in Fig. 9-4. You will hear the ticking very faintly or might not hear it at all. This is because the ticking of the clock is a high-pitched sound. High-pitched sounds are made up mostly of short waves, and short waves don't bend much.

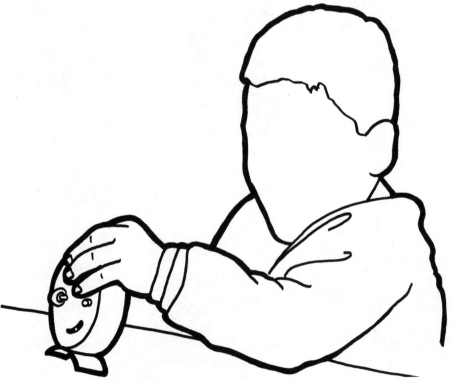

Fig. 9-1. Place a ticking clock on a table.

Fig. 9-2. *Stand about four feet away from the table.*

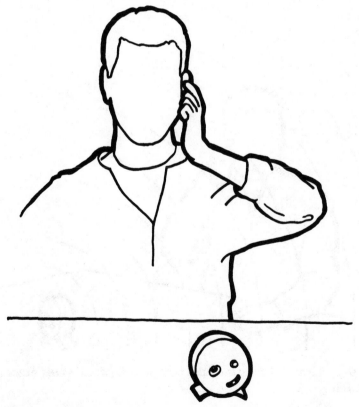

Fig. 9-3. *Plug one ear with your finger.*

When you stood facing the clock, the short sound waves were able to enter your ear, but when you turned to the side with the plugged ear facing the clock, your head blocked off the sound waves, or made a shadow where most of the short waves were unable to travel. Low pitched sounds have longer waves that bend easily.

When you hear a marching band, you can hear the music from around a corner. Most of the sound you hear, however, is from the low-pitched instruments like the drums and trombones. The longer waves will bend around corners. Higher-pitched instruments like the flute, will not be heard until you can see them because they produce shorter waves that don't bend easily.

Fig. 9-4. *A sound shadow is created because high-pitched sound waves do not bend easily.*

Experiment 10

The Humming Stick

Using the hammer and nail, make a hole near one end of the piece of wood (Fig. 10-1). Thread one end of the string through the hole and tie it securely. Tie the other end of the string to the round stick (Fig. 10-2). Get outside in a clear area and, holding the round stick, whirl the

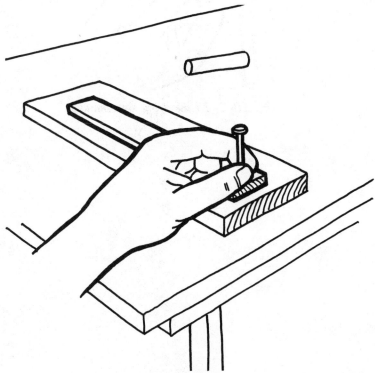

Fig. 10-1. Make a hole in one end of the piece of wood.

piece of wood over your head (Fig. 10-3). It will make a strange hum-ming noise.

The piece of wood rotates as it spins. This causes it to travel at an irregular speed and move different volumes of air at a varying fre-quency. This irregular pattern of vibrations produces noises such as sirens, while a regular frequency of vibrations might be musical.

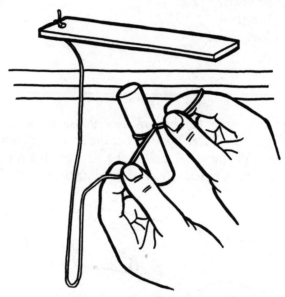

Fig. 10-2. *Tie the string to the handle.*

Fig. 10-3. *The whirling stick makes a humming sound.*

Experiment 11

The Doppler Effect

> **Materials**
>
> ☐ an approaching
>   train, fire truck,
>   or ambulance

Listen to the sound of a train or an emergency vehicle (Fig. 11-1). As it passes, notice the difference in the pitch of the sound. Then keep listening as it goes away. The pitch will appear to change (Fig. 11-2). This apparent change in pitch is called the Doppler effect after the German physicist Christian Doppler, who described the principle in 1842.

Fig. 11-1. Listen to the sound of a moving object.

The pitch, or frequency, of a train whistle seems to sound higher as the train comes closer, then becomes lower as it goes away. This is because, as the train approaches, the sound waves are pushed closer together. More sound waves strike your ear each second. The frequency is higher so the pitch seems higher. When the train passes and starts moving away, the sound waves are stretched apart. Fewer sound waves strike your ear each second. The frequency is lower and the pitch will sound lower. The whistle actually has only one pitch. The Doppler effect is the apparent change in frequency of sound, light, or radio waves caused by motion.

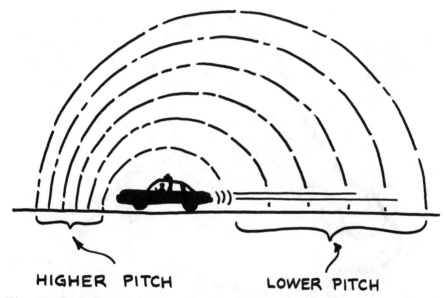

HIGHER PITCH   **LOWER PITCH**

Fig. 11-2. *As the object passes, the sound will go from a high pitch to a low pitch.*

Experiment 12

Why Seashells Produce Unusual Sounds

Materials

- ☐ seashell
- ☐ curved vase
- ☐ tall thin glass
- ☐ cardboard tube

Fig. 12-1. *Compare the sounds of different shaped objects.*

Place the different objects next to your ear and notice the sounds each one makes (Fig. 12-1). Sound is produced by vibration. The type of sound an object makes is determined by the material the object is made of, along with its size and shape. The walls of a seashell are made to vibrate by particles of air striking the outside of the shell. This causes the air inside to vibrate. The spiral shape bounces the vibrations from one surface to another and are amplified by the shell. The oceanlike sound produced by the shell is made when the sound waves are amplified and reflected from the curved surfaces.

Experiment 13

Materials

☐ clean, dry comb
☐ piece of wax paper

How to Make a Musical Comb

Fold the wax paper in half and place the comb inside the fold (Fig. 13-1). Hold the comb at each end, pressing the paper against the teeth of the comb (Fig. 13-2). Gently press your lips against the paper and hum (Fig. 13-3). You will hear an unusual sound. Try a song and you will see you can play a tune. The humming causes the paper to vibrate. This makes the paper vibrate against the teeth of the comb and produces a buzzing sound.

Fig. 13-1. *Fold a piece of wax paper.*

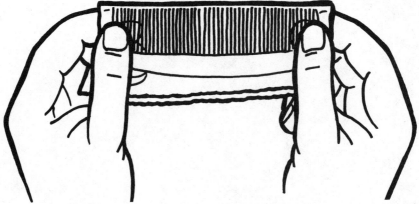

Fig. 13-2. *Place the comb inside the wax paper.*

Fig. 13-3. *Place your lips against the wax paper and hum a tune.*

Experiment 14

A Noisy Balloon

Fill the balloon with air. Hold it under one arm and against your side with the opening pointing to the front (Fig. 14-1). Stretch the opening from the side while you release the air (Fig. 14-2). Additional pressure can be added by pressing your arm against your side. By changing the stretching and the pressure, a variety of strange sounds can be produced.

Fig. 14-1. *Fill the balloon with air, then hold the balloon under one arm.*

When the air is forced through the stretched opening, the rubber vibrates and makes the air come out in a series of waves. Normally, the waves come out in an irregular pattern and this produces noise. But if you make the waves come out in a series of regular patterns, you will produce musical sounds.

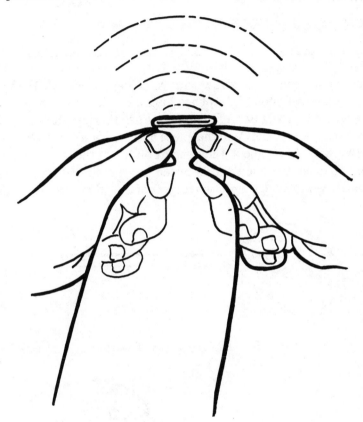

Fig. 14-2. *Stretching the opening will change the sound.*

Experiment 15

Musical Straw

Flatten one end of the straw with your fingers (Fig. 15-1). Cut the strip of cardboard about 1½ inches long and wide enough so that it will wedge into the flat part of the straw. Push this into the straw (Fig. 15-2). About halfway between this piece and the open end of the straw, make two small holes about 1 inch apart on top of the straw using the scissor. Hold the flattened end between the thumb and finger of one hand and cover the holes with two fingers of the other hand (Fig. 15-3).

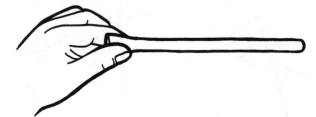

Fig. 15-1. Flatten one end of the straw.

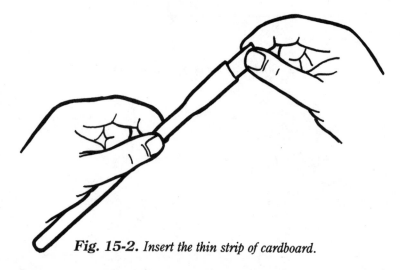

Fig. 15-2. Insert the thin strip of cardboard.

Blow into the flat end applying a little pressure between your thumb and finger (Fig. 15-4). With a little practice, musical notes can be produced.

The thin cardboard vibrates and makes the sound. The pitch is determined by how much air comes out the end of the straw, which can be changed by opening and closing the holes.

Fig. 15-3. *Make two holes in the straw.*

Fig. 15-4. *The pitch can be changed by opening and closing the holes.*

Experiment 16

Straw Whistle

Materials

☐ **drinking straw**
☐ **scissors**

Flatten about one inch of the end of the straw (Fig. 16-1). If the straw is plastic, you'll have to bend and kink it some to get the end flat. Next, cut off both corners so that the flattened end has three equal sides (Fig. 16-2). Place this end just inside your lips and blow (Fig. 16-3). It might take a little practice and you might have to position the straw to one side of your lips, but soon you will make a musical sound. Your lips will tingle. Notice the pitch of the note. Now, snip off a couple inches from the other end of the straw while you'll still blowing (Fig. 16-4), and suddenly the pitch will go higher.

When you blow through a regular straw, the air flows smoothly out the end and no sound is heard. With the end flattened and the corners trimmed, the straw vibrates. This is what made your lips tingle.

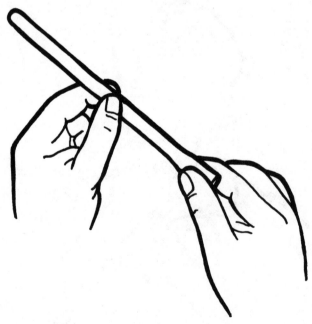

Fig. 16-1. Flatten one end of the straw.

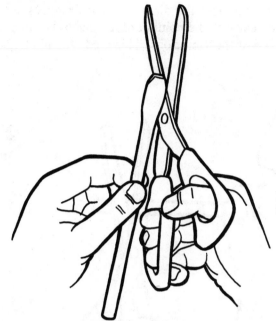

Fig. 16-2. *Trim off the corners.*

Fig. 16-3. *Place the flattened end just inside your lips and blow.*

The vibrating straw vibrates the air inside and produces the sound. When the end was cut off, the column of air inside became shorter, increasing the speed of the vibrations. This made the pitch higher.

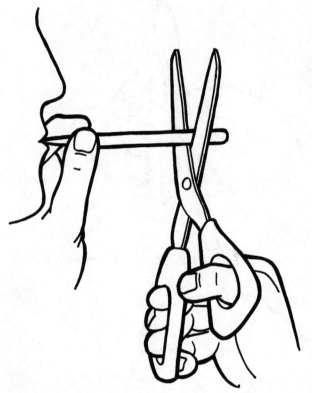

Fig. 16-4. Cut a little off the end and notice the change in pitch.

Experiment 17

Materials

☐ **large drinking straw**
☐ **X-Acto knife**

Changing Tones with a Straw

Carefully make a fine cut across the middle of the straw with the X-Acto knife. Never cut against yourself. Don't cut all the way through. Bend the straw at the cut and flatten one of the ends (Fig. 17-1). Now, blow through the flattened end and hold your finger over the other end (Fig. 17-2). Adjust the angle of the bend until you hear a tone. The bend might be pointing almost straight down. When you hear the tone, remove your finger from the end of the straw. The tone will go to the next higher note (Fig. 17-3).

When the sound was first made, it was caused by the vibrations of the air in the one part of the straw. When you removed your finger, this opened the other part of the straw and the vibrations from this part were added to the first vibrations. This produced the higher tone.

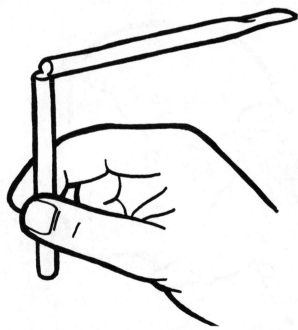

Fig. 17-1. Make a cut in the straw, then flatten one end and bend the straw.

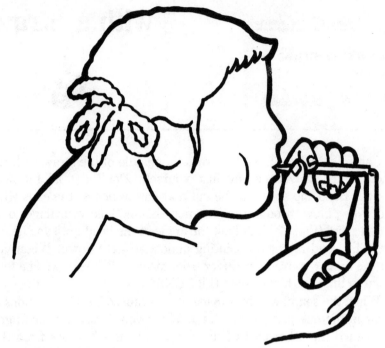

Fig. 17-2. *Change the angle of the bend until you hear a tone.*

Fig. 17-3. *Remove your finger and the tone will change.*

Experiment 18

Materials

- ☐ **8 tall drinking glasses**
- ☐ **pitcher of water**
- ☐ **pencil**

Water and the Pitch of Glasses

Arrange the glasses in a row and fill the first one nearly to the top with water (Fig. 18-1). Tap it with the pencil and notice the sound. Now, fill the second glass with water but not as full as the first. Tap it with the pencil and compare that sound with the sound from the first glass (Fig. 18-2). It will have a higher pitch. Raise or lower the water level of the second glass to make the next highest note from the first glass. You might find the water level only about 1/4 inch lower than the first glass. Repeat the steps with the remaining glasses, with each glass having a little less water (Fig. 18-3). It will take some experimenting to find the proper water levels, but when you have them tuned, you will be able to make musical sounds.

Fig. 18-1. *Fill the first glass almost full.*

The tapping pencil causes the glass to vibrate and produce the sound. The water dampens, or slows these vibrations. So the less water in the glass, the faster the glass vibrates and the higher the pitch. This can be simply demonstrated by slowly dragging your fingernail across the cover of a book. Notice the pitch. Now do it again, only a little faster. The pitch is higher. As the speed is increased, the vibrations are faster and the pitch becomes higher.

Fig. 18-2. Tap the glasses with a pencil.

Fig. 18-3. *The glass with the least amount of water has the highest pitch.*

Experiment 19

Musical Bottles

Materials

- ☐ **4 empty bottles, the same size**
- ☐ **pencil**
- ☐ **water**

Pour a small amount of water into one of the bottles. Fill the second bottle with a little more water than the first (Fig. 19-1). Fill the third bottle with more water than the second bottle, and the fourth bottle should be almost full. Now, blow across the top of the first bottle (Fig. 19-2). Aim the stream of air so that it hits just inside the edge on

Fig. 19-1. Fill the bottles with different amounts of water.

the other side of the opening. Notice the sound. Blow across the second, third and fourth bottles. Notice how the pitch became higher (Fig. 19-3). Now, tap the first bottle with the pencil (Fig. 19-4). Listen to the sound. Tap the second, third, and fourth bottles. This time the pitch went lower.

When you blew across the top of the bottle, a wave of compressed air travelled down the inside of the bottle. It struck the bottom and was reflected back up toward the opening. When it left the opening, the compression expanded, sending another wave down toward the bottom of the bottle. The compressed and expanded waves travel up and down the inside of the bottle passing right through each other. When these waves reach the opening of the bottle, they force the stream of air from your lips to swing back and forth across the opening. The stream of air is vibrating. When this vibrating stream strikes the surrounding air, it produces the sound. The bottle with the least amount of water will produce the lowest pitch because the waves travel farther inside the bottle. The more water in the bottle, the

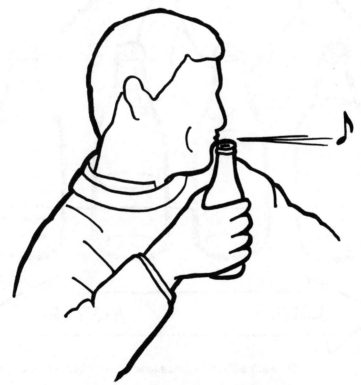

Fig. 19-2. *Blow across the top of each bottle.*

shorter the distance. This makes the waves return very quickly and makes the stream of air vibrate faster, producing a higher pitch.

When the bottles were tapped with the pencil, the sound was produced by the vibrating glass. The water slowed, or dampened, the vibrations. So the more water in the bottle, the slower the glass vibrated and the lower the pitch.

Fig. 19-3. *The bottle with the least amount of water has the lowest pitch.*

Fig. 19-4. *When the bottles are tapped with a pencil, the bottle with the least amount of water has the highest pitch.*

Experiment 20

The Musical Glass

Materials

- ☐ **thin drinking glass**
- ☐ **vinegar**
- ☐ **water**

Pour a little water into the glass and add a few drops of vinegar (Fig. 20-1). Next, dip one of your fingers into the water and slowly rub it around the rim of the glass (Figs. 20-2 and 20-3). Use a smooth, steady motion. You might have to dip your finger back into the water a few times, but within two or three tries, you will be able to produce musical sounds.

The vinegar is used to remove the oil from the fingertip and the rim of the glass. The moving finger produces vibrations in the glass the same way a violin bow produces vibrations in the strings of a violin. Using different sizes of glasses and different amounts of water will change the pitch of the sound.

Fig. 20-1. Pour a small amount of water into the glass, then add a little vinegar.

Fig. 20-2. Wet the end of your finger.

Fig. 20-3. Rub your finger around the rim.

Experiment 21

Jerky Vibrations

Materials

- [ ] pencil
- [ ] piece of thread (about 3 feet long)
- [ ] drinking glass or cardboard tube

Tie one end of the thread tightly around the middle of the glass or tube (Fig. 21-1). Tie the other end of the string into a small loop and slide the pencil through this loop (Fig. 21-2). Hold the glass upright next to your ear, and holding the pencil, stretch the thread out until it is taut. Now, very slowly, rotate the pencil (Fig. 21-3). You will hear a strange noise coming from the glass.

The pencil rubbing the thread inside the loop makes the thread vibrate in a jerky pattern. This causes the glass to vibrate in an irregular pattern and makes the surrounding air vibrate. The vibrating air carries the sound to your ear.

Fig. 21-1. Tie the thread around the glass.

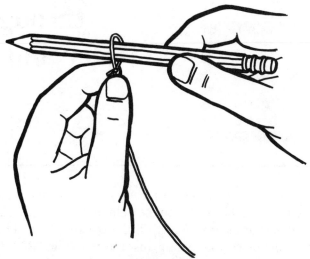

Fig. 21-2. *Insert the pencil into the loop.*

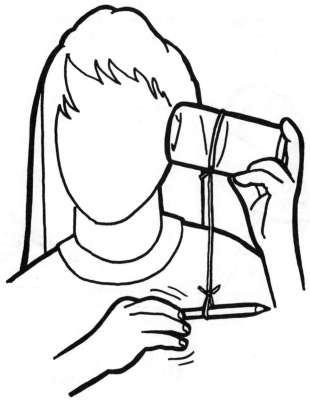

Fig. 21-3. *Stretch the thread and twist the pencil.*

Experiment 22

How Sound Travels through Water and Wood

Materials

☐ wooden table
☐ metal bucket
☐ comb
☐ water

Place your ear against the surface of one end of the table and ask someone to tap the other end with the point of a pencil (Fig. 22-1). You will hear the sound clearly. Now, fill the bucket about three-fourths full of water and place your ear against the side (Fig. 22-2). Lower the comb about halfway down into the water and rub your fingernail across the teeth (Fig. 22-3). Again, the sound is easily carried to your ear.

Normally, we hear sounds brought to us through vibrations in the air, but sound can travel very well through wood, water, even our teeth and the bones in your head.

Fig. 22-1. The tapping pencil is easily heard.

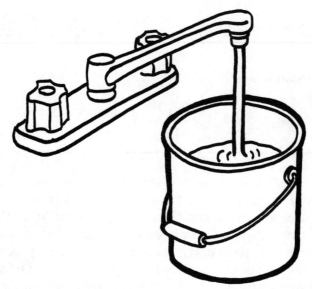

Fig. 22-2. *Fill the bucket with water.*

Fig. 22-3. *Rub your fingernail across the comb and listen to side of the bucket.*

Experiment 23

Sound Vibrations through Our Teeth

Tie a small loop in one end of the thread and tie the other end tightly around the middle of the pencil (Fig. 23-1). Hold the pencil crossways in your teeth and place a finger in the loop. Stretch the thread out taut and pluck it with one finger (Fig. 23-2). You will hear a musical note. The pitch of this note can be changed by increasing or lowering the tension on the thread. The plucked thread transmits the sound to your teeth. The teeth are solidly connected to the bones in your head and this provides an easy path for sound to travel to the nerves in your ear.

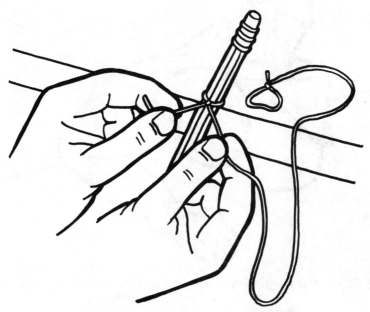

Fig. 23-1. *Tie the thread around the pencil.*

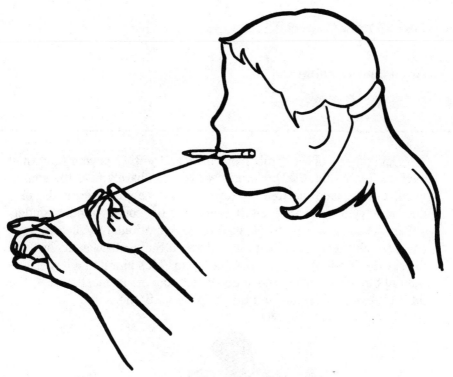

Fig. 23-2. Sound vibrations travel through your teeth to your ear.

Experiment 24

The Vibrating Comb

Materials

☐ comb
☐ wooden door or table

Hold the end of the comb in one hand and softly run your fingernail over the teeth (Fig. 24-1). Notice that you can barely hear the sound. Now, firmly place the free end of the comb against the middle of a door and try it again (Fig. 24-2). This time the sound is much louder. When the teeth were first stroked, their vibrations travelled to your ear through the surrounding air, but when the comb was against the door, the vibrations also went to the wood. This vibrated a larger volume of air, which made the sound much louder. In most homes, the interior doors are hollow and this helps amplify the sound.

Fig. 24-1. *Stroke the teeth of the comb in free air.*

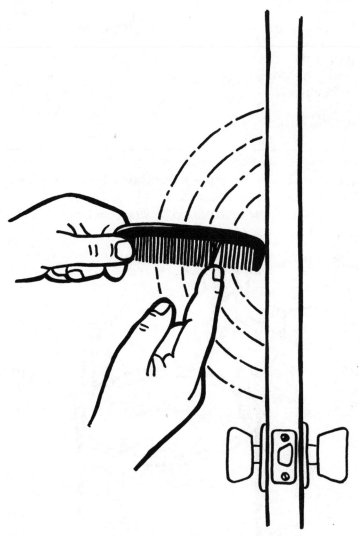

Fig. 24-2. *Stroke the teeth of the comb touching the door.*

Experiment 25

Materials

- [ ] empty pop can
- [ ] 2 nails and a hammer
- [ ] small rubber band

Rubber Band and Musical Pitch

Make sure the can is empty and dry, then turn it upside down and carefully drive the nails about halfway into each side of the bottom (Fig. 25-1). Stretch the rubber band between the two nails and pluck it

Fig. 25-1. *Force the nails halfway into the can.*

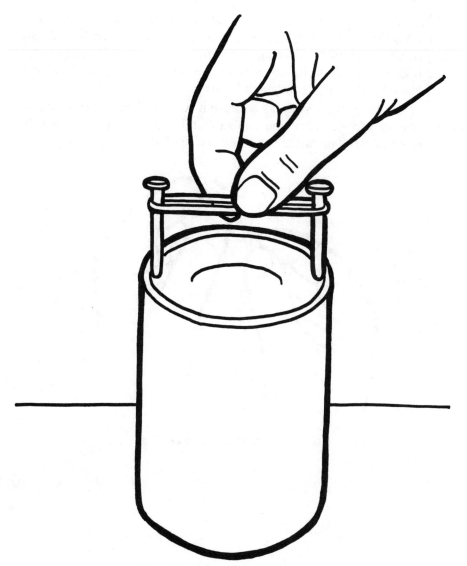

Fig. 25-2. *Pluck the rubber band.*

(Fig. 25-2). Notice the sound from the can. Remove the rubber band, tie a knot in one end and stretch it between the nails again (Fig. 25-3). Now, pluck the rubber band again and notice the sound. The pitch will be higher (Fig. 25-4). Remove the rubber band, tie another knot and try it again. Each time, the pitch becomes higher.

The rubber band vibrates because it was plucked and this makes the sound waves. When the rubber band was stretched tighter, it vibrated faster. The faster the vibration, the higher the pitch.

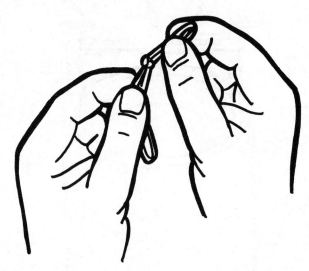

Fig. 25-3. *Shorten the rubber band.*

Fig. 25-3. *Pluck the rubber band. The pitch is higher.*

Experiment 26

How to Make a One-String Bass Viol (Fiddle)

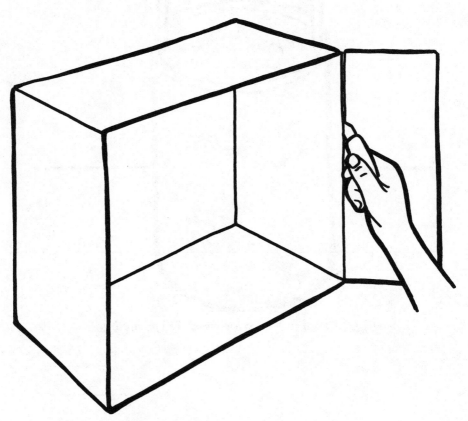

Fig. 26-1. *Carefully remove the flaps from the box.*

66

Remove the flaps from the top of the cardboard box (Fig. 26-1). Make a small hole in the box and thread the end of the string through the hole. Tie a pencil or stick inside the box to keep the string from pulling through the cardboard (Fig. 26-2). Place the box on the floor with the open end down. Now, stand the broom upside down with the end of the handle on the box. Stretch the string up to the other end of the handle and tie it securely (Fig. 26-3). Pull back on the broom with one hand and pluck the string with the other as shown in Fig. 26-4.

The pitch of the sound can be changed by how hard you pull on the broom. The vibrating string causes the box to vibrate a large volume of air. The tighter the string is stretched, the faster it vibrates and the higher the pitch.

Fig. 26-2. *Tie the pencil to the string.*

Fig. 26-3. *Tie the string to the broom.*

Fig. 26-4. *Keep the string tight with the broom and pluck the string.*

Experiment 27

Baking Pan Amplifier

Tie one end of the string to the handle of one of the forks (Fig. 27-1). Tie the other end of the string through the hole in the end of the pan (Fig. 27-2). Place the pan upside down on a table or counter top. Have the end with the string sticking over the edge so that the fork is suspended below (Fig. 27-3). Now, lift the fork by the string and tap it with the other fork as shown in Fig. 27-4. Notice the sound. Release the string so that the fork will hang from the pan. Tap the fork again (Fig. 27-5). notice the increase in loudness.

The first sound was made by the vibrations of the fork alone. The second sound was also made by vibrations from the fork, but the string carried the vibrations to the pan. The pan vibrated a larger amount of air, amplifying the sound.

Fig. 27-1. Tie the string to the fork.

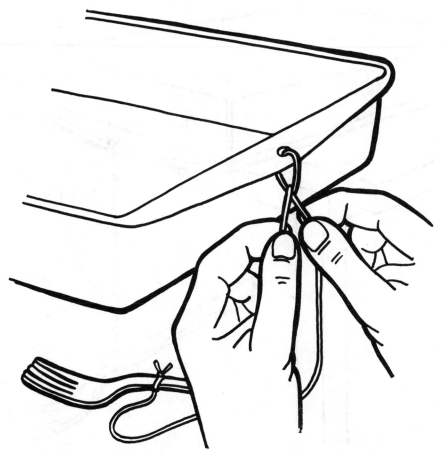

Fig. 27-2. *Tie the string to the pan.*

Fig. 27-3. *Suspend the fork over the edge of the table.*

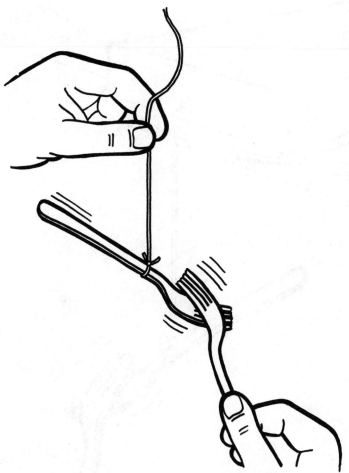

Fig. 27-4. *Lift the string and tap the fork.*

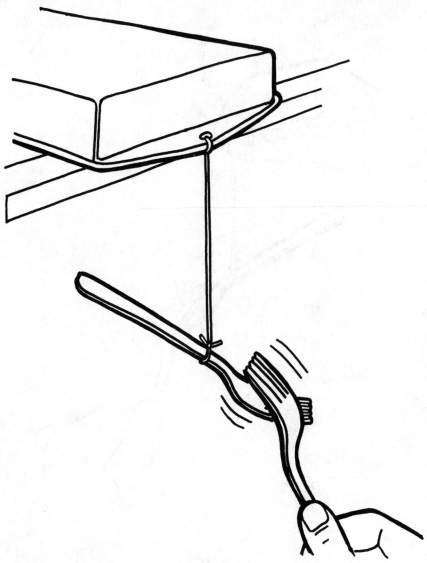

Fig. 27-5. *Release the string and tap the fork again.*

Experiment 28

Materials

- ☐ thin glass
- ☐ fork
- ☐ knife
- ☐ wooden table

Drinking Glass Amplifier

Place the glass near the edge of the table and hold your ear a few inches above the opening (Fig. 28-1). Grip the handle of the fork firmly and tap the other end with the handle of the knife (Fig. 28-2). It might take two or three tries, but you can make the fork ring. When it does, touch the handle to the table a couple of feet from the glass as shown in Fig. 28-3. Instantly, the sound of the ringing fork will be coming from the glass.

Fig. 28-1. *Place the glass on the table.*

When the fork was first struck, the sound is heard only faintly. It travelled directly to your ear through vibrations in the air. When the fork touched the table, the vibrations travelled through the wood to the glass where the sound was amplified.

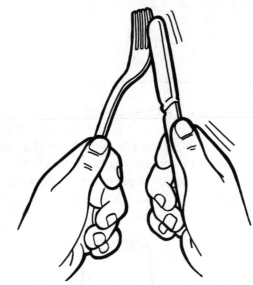

Fig. 28-2. *Tap the fork to make it ring.*

Fig. 28-3. *Touch the fork to the table and listen to the glass.*

Experiment 29

Sound Travelling through a Water Pipe

Materials

☐ kitchen sink
☐ bathroom sink

Open the cabinet doors below the kitchen sink where there are exposed water pipes and listen (Fig. 29-1). If no water is running in the house, the pipes will be silent. Now go into the bathroom, turn on the cold water faucet at the sink and let a small stream of water run. Return to the kitchen and now listen to the pipes below the sink. You

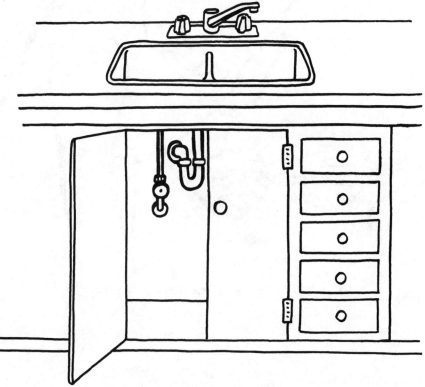

Fig. 29-1. Water pipes below the sink.

will be able to hear the sound of the water running in the bathroom. Water pipes are good conductors of sound. Messages can even be sent from one room to another by tapping the pipes with a small piece of iron (Fig. 29-2). Listen to the tapping by placing a ruler between the pipe and your head (Fig. 29-3).

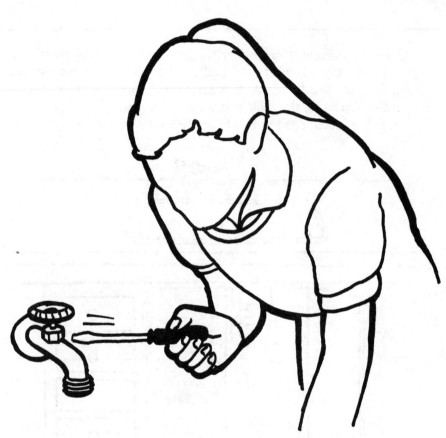

Fig. 29-2. *Tap a water pipe with a piece of metal.*

Fig. 29-3. *Sound can be heard through the ruler.*

Experiment 30

Materials

- ☐ cardboard tube from paper towels
- ☐ large glass or jar
- ☐ water

Resonance and Sympathetic Vibrations

Fill the glass about three-fourths full of water. Lower one end of the jar a couple of inches into the water (Fig. 30-1). Hold the jar in one hand and the tube in the other. Whistle or hum a steady note

Fig. 30-1. Pour water into the jar then lower the end of the tube into the water.

across the open end of the tube (Fig. 30-2). At the same time, raise and lower the jar a little and notice the sound. At one point, the sound will suddenly become louder. This is when the column of air inside the tube is of the correct volume and is vibrating at the same frequency as the whistle across the end of the tube. The vibrations of the column of air strengthens the vibrations of the sound making it louder.

Fig. 30-2. *Raise and lower the jar while you hum a note.*

Experiment 31

Bottle Resonance

Place the opening of one of the bottles close to your ear. Ask someone to stand near you and blow a stream of air across the opening of the other bottle (Fig. 31-1). It might take several tries for them to get a strong sound from their bottle, and you might have to adjust the angle of the bottle you're holding, but when this is done just right, you will hear the same sound coming from your bottle as the one made on the other bottle.

When the other person blew across the mouth of one bottle, it made a sound. This sound is made up of vibrations that travelled through the air to the bottle you held to your ear. The vibrations made your bottle vibrate like the other one. The bottles were in harmony. They acted in resonance.

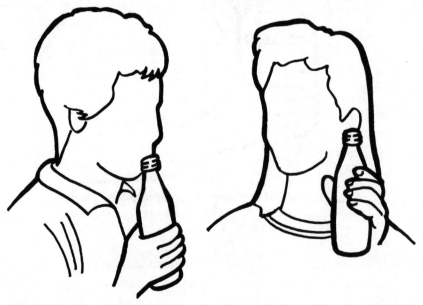

Fig. 31-1. Blow across the bottle and make a sound come from the other bottle.

Experiment 32

Sympathetic Vibrations

Materials

☐ **2 thin drinking glasses the same size**
☐ **spoon**
☐ **paper clip**
☐ **water**

Fill each glass about one-third full of water. Try to have the same amount in each glass (Fig. 32-1). Tap each glass with the edge of the spoon. If there is any difference in the notes, add a little water to one until they both sound the same. Place the glasses about four inches apart. Straighten the paper clip and place it across the top of one of the glasses (Fig. 32-2). Tap the other glass with the spoon and watch the paper clip closely. You will see the paper clip move a little (Fig. 32-3).

Fig. 32-1. Fill two glasses with the same amount of water.

This happened because the glass had sympathetic vibrations with the glass you tapped. The two glasses are in resonance. The water levels were filled to the level that caused both glasses to sound the same note. This means that they both vibrated at the same rate, or frequency. When two objects vibrate at the same frequency and one is struck, it will cause the other one to vibrate at the same rate, only weaker. A string plucked on one musical instrument can cause a similar string on a nearby instrument to vibrate.

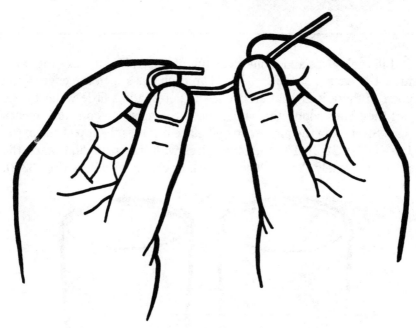

Fig. 32-2. *Straighten the paper clip.*

Fig. 32-3. *The paper clip will move slightly.*

Experiment 33

How to Mellow Sound

Fig. 33-1. *Hum a note and move the jar in front of your mouth. In one place the sound will mellow.*

Hum a note or tune and slowly bring the opening of the jar in front of your mouth (Fig. 33-1). Move the jar away then bring it back. Notice the change in the sound. At some point, the sound mellowed. Try the same thing with the oat box and the cardboard tube (Figs. 33-2 and 33-3). Each one will produce a little different sound. One will amplify the lower tones while another will amplify the higher tones. The sound of your humming created vibrations of different frequencies. When they were aimed into the jar, or tube, the sound waves were reflected. Some of the reflected, lower frequency, sound waves combined with the original low frequency waves. This amplified the lower frequency sounds making them soft and mellow.

Fig. 33-2. *Repeat the steps with a round box.*

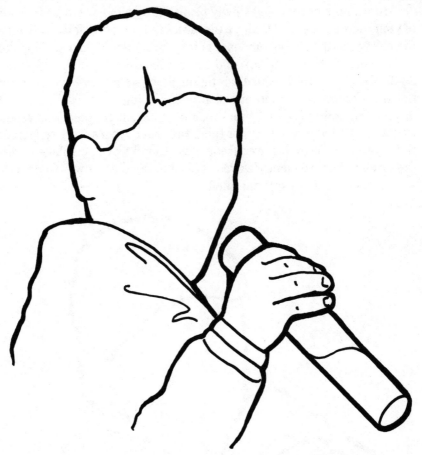

Fig. 33-3. *Try to mellow the sound with a tube.*

Experiment 34   Deadening Sound

Materials

- ☐ string
- ☐ fork
- ☐ toothpicks or small pieces of twisted paper
- ☐ knife

Tie one end of the string around the handle of the fork (Fig. 34-1). Hold the other end of the string in one hand and tap the prongs of the fork with the knife (Fig. 34-2). Notice the ringing sound. Now, wedge the toothpick, or the paper, between the prongs of the fork and tap it again (Figs. 34-3 and 34-4). The sound now is deadened.

When the fork was first tapped, the prongs were free to vibrate and make the sound waves. When the toothpicks were wedged in place, however, the vibrations were dampened and could not produce the ringing sound.

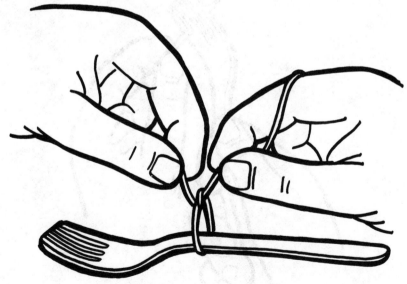

Fig. 34-1. *Tie the string around the fork.*

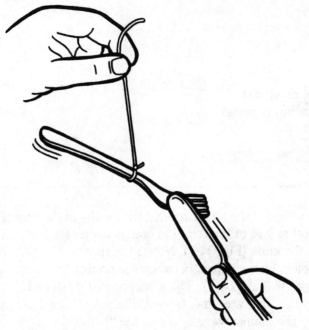

Fig. 34-2. *Tap the fork and notice the sound.*

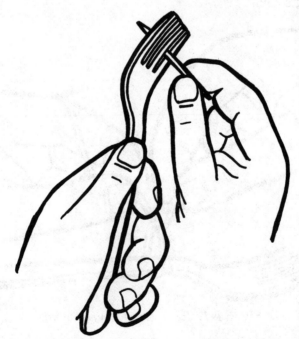

Fig. 34-3. *Wedge toothpicks between the prongs.*

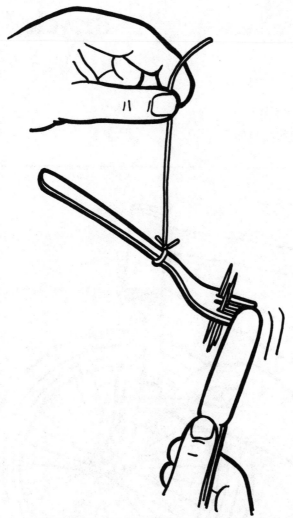

Fig. 34-4. *Tap the fork. The sound is deadened.*

Experiment 35

Pitch from a Bicycle Wheel

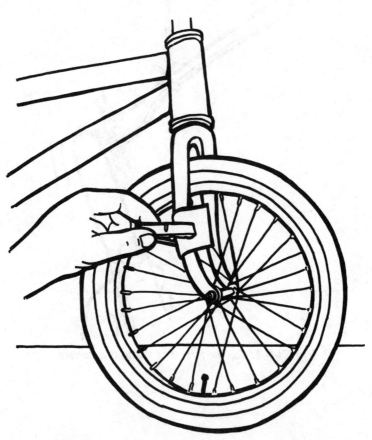

Fig. 35-1. *Use a clothespin to hold the card in place.*

Wrap one end of the cardboard around the frame of the bicycle. Adjust it so that the other end of the cardboard sticks into the wheel far enough to touch the spokes. Clamp it to the frame with the clothespin (Fig. 35-1). Now, ride the bicycle. It will sound like it has a motor (Fig. 35-2). The faster you peddle, the faster the cardboard vibrates. The faster the cardboard vibrates, the higher the pitch of the sound.

Fig. 35-2. *The spokes cause the card to vibrate.*

Experiment 36

Materials

☐ **large blade of grass or strip of paper**

How to Make a Grass Whistle

Hold one end of the blade of grass between your thumb and the first finger of one hand (Fig. 36-1). Now, lay the grass along the side of that thumb (Fig. 36-2). Place your hands together with both thumbs lined up holding the grass. The grass blade should be stretched flat with a small opening between the thumbs. Blow through this opening (Fig. 36-3). With a little practice, you will be able to make a musical tone.

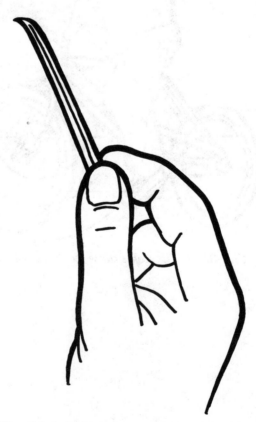

Fig. 36-1. Hold the blade of grass in one hand.

Opening and closing the hollow of your hands will change the pitch of the tone (Fig. 36-4). When you blow across the blade of grass, it vibrates. This vibration produces the sound. Opening and closing your hands changes the patterns of the sound waves.

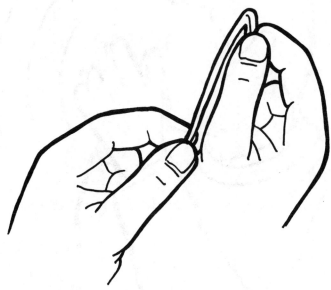

Fig. 36-2. *Place the blade alongside your thumb.*

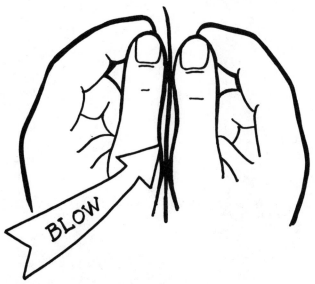

Fig. 36-3. *Place your thumbs together and blow through the opening.*

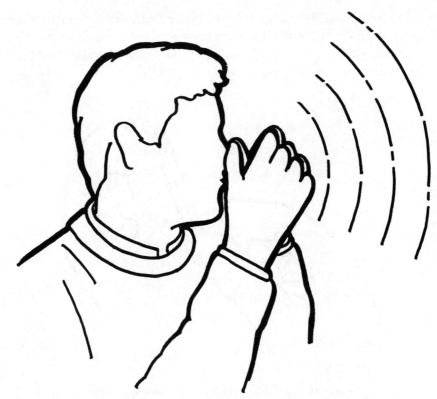

Fig. 36-4. *The vibrating blade of grass produces the sound.*

Experiment 37

Materials

- [ ] metal baking pan
- [ ] about 8 rubber bands

How to Make a Rubber Band Harp

Stretch about eight rubber bands around the pan. Place them about an inch apart (Fig. 37-1). Stretch the rubber tighter to raise the pitch. Tie a knot in the end when you get the right sound or use different sized rubber bands. After you have them all tuned, pluck the strands of rubber like a harp. You will be able to make musical sounds. The rubber vibrates when it is plucked, producing the sounds. These vibrations are amplified by the pan.

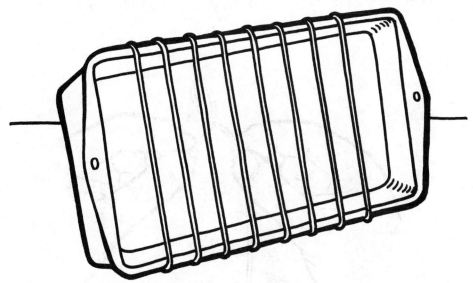

Fig. 37-1. Place rubber bands around a pan to make a harp.

Experiment 38

How to Make a Spoon Chime

Materials

☐ spoon
☐ string (about three feet long)

Tie small loops in each end of the string (Fig. 38-1). Tie the middle of the string around the spoon (Fig. 38-2). Put a finger through each loop and then into each ear. Lean over and let the suspended spoon gently bump the edge of a table or chair as shown in Fig. 38-3. The sound will be like a large church bell ringing. Try a fork or a knife to hear different tones. Try a thin copper wire instead of the string. The sound will be even louder.

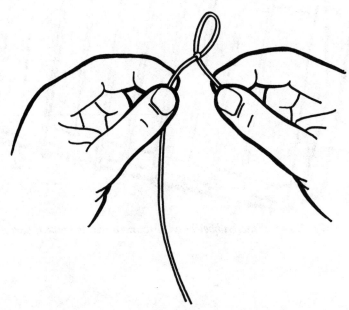

Fig. 38-1. *Tie a loop in each end of the string.*

The vibrations from the spoon travel up the string to your eardrums. There, nerves transmit the sound waves to the brain, which changes them to sound. Because of the shape of the spoon, its curves and different thicknesses, a variety of sounds are produced. Some of these are produced by overtones, or partial tones. These are higher tones that are heard with the basic tones. Overtones vibrate at a frequency that is an exact multiple of the frequency of the basic tone.

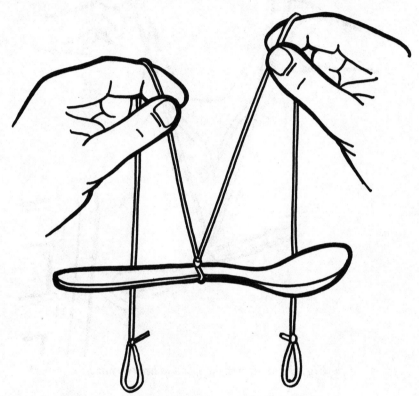

Fig. 38-2. Attach the spoon to the middle of the string.

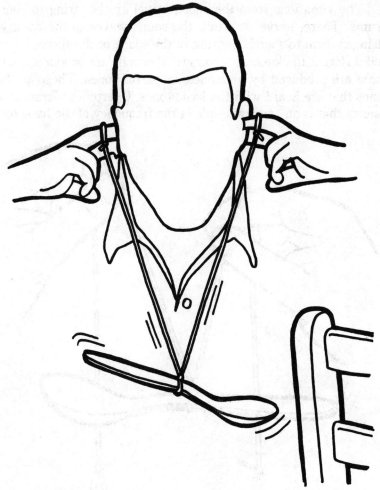

Fig. 38-3. *Bump the spoon to hear a chime.*

Experiment 39

How to Make Chimes with Flatware

Materials

- ☐ string (about 4 feet long)
- ☐ knife
- ☐ fork
- ☐ spoon

Tie a small loop in each end of the string, then fold the string in half, placing the loops together (see Fig. 39-1). This gives you the exact middle of the string. Tie the middle of the string to the handle of

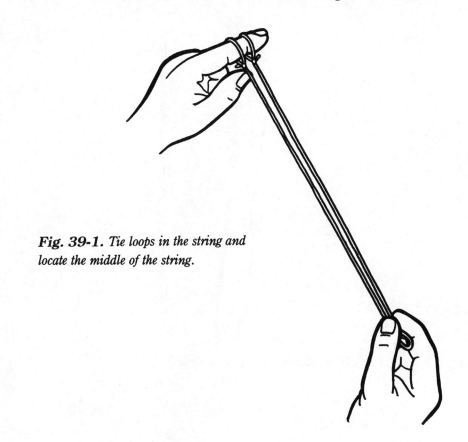

Fig. 39-1. *Tie loops in the string and locate the middle of the string.*

the knife. Attach the string to the end of the handle so that the blade hangs down (Fig. 39-2). Now, unfold the string and tie the fork and spoon on each side of the knife (Fig. 39-3). Tie them about three inches apart. Place a finger in each loop then put the end of your finger in each ear. Lean forward a little, suspending the knife, fork, and spoon in the air as shown in Fig. 39-4. Move your head from side to side and you will hear the beautiful sound of chimes.

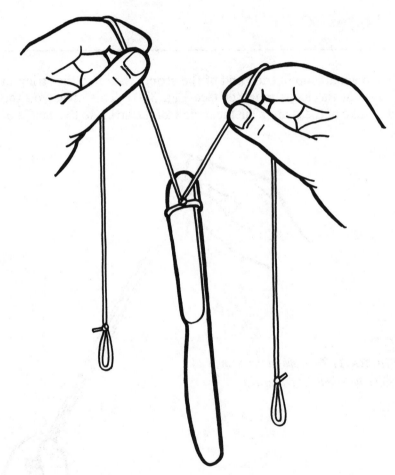

Fig. 39-2. Attach the knife to the middle of the string.

Because each piece is free to vibrate, when they bump each other the sound rings longer. The vibrations travel up the string to your ears where the sound is amplified. Because the string is soft, it dampens some of the harsh sounds making the chimes more mellow. Each piece vibrates at a regular frequency and this causes the sounds to be musical. Vibrations at irregular frequencies make noise.

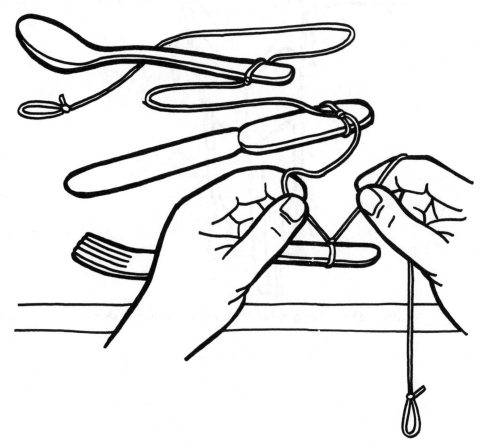

Fig. 39-3. *Attach the fork and spoon on each side of the knife.*

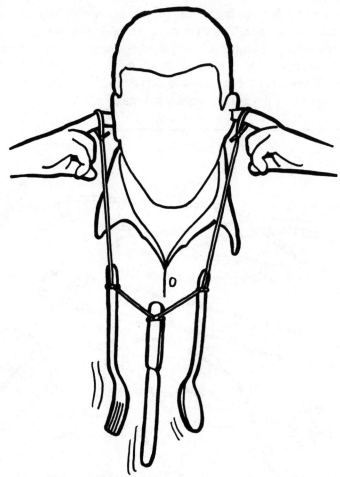

Fig. 39-4. *Move your head from side to side to hear chimes.*

Experiment 40

How to Make a Stethoscope

Materials

- [ ] length of small garden hose (about 18 inches long)
- [ ] funnel
- [ ] wind up or electric clock

Insert the small end of the funnel into one end of the hose (Fig. 40-1). Place the opening of the other end of the hose against your ear. Try putting it against your heart. You probably can't hear the beating of your heart, but the hum of an electric clock or the ticking of a wind-up clock will be much louder.

Fig. 40-1. *Insert the funnel in one end of the hose.*

Place the clock on the table about a foot away and listen (Fig. 40-2). The vibrations of the little electric motor inside the clock causes the air inside the funnel to vibrate. This vibrates the trapped air inside the hose where it travels to your ear. The vibrations are concentrated enough so that you are able to hear small sounds that you wouldn't hear in the open air.

Fig. 40-2. *You can hear small sounds from the tube.*

Experiment 41

How to Make a Speaking Tube

Materials

☐ garden hose
☐ 2 people

Stretch the hose out to its full length. Blow hard through one end to make sure the hose is empty of water. Now ask someone to speak in one end while you listen in the other end (Fig. 41-1). You will have to

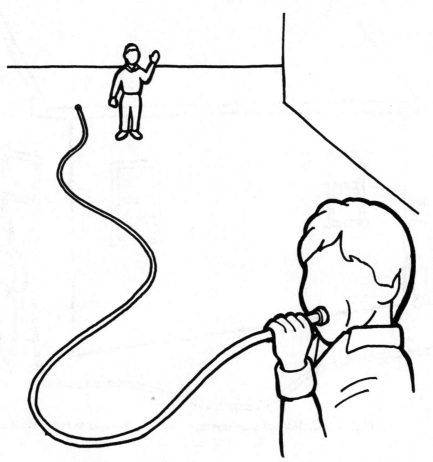

Fig. 41-1. *Make sure the hose is empty of water.*

take turns talking and listening but you will be able to hear each other clearly. You can still hear even when you bend the hose around a corner (Fig. 41-2). Just don't put any kinks in the hose.

The sound waves are trapped inside the hose. This concentrates the vibrations so that you can easily hear the person at the other end. This was a common method of sending orders from the bridge of a ship to the engine room.

Fig. 41-2. *You can hear someone speaking in the other end of the hose.*

Experiment 42

Materials

- [ ] cardboard tube from paper towels
- [ ] sheet of paper
- [ ] scissors
- [ ] glue
- [ ] transparent tape

How to Make a Megaphone

Cut the paper into the shape of a funnel (Fig. 42-1). Make the opening in the small end large enough to fit around the cardboard tube. Use tape to hold the seams of the funnel together (Fig. 42-2).

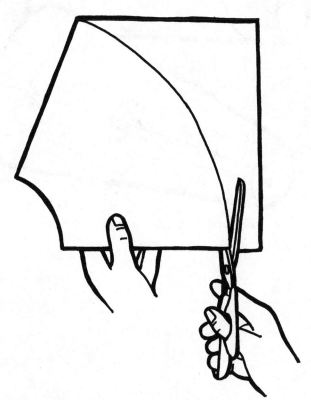

Fig. 42-1. *Cut a funnel from the paper.*

Insert one end of the cardboard tube a couple of inches into the small end of the funnel. Glue the funnel to the tube as shown in Fig. 42-3. When the glue has dried, ask someone to listen some distance away while you speak softly into the open end of the tube (Fig. 42-4). Aim the funnel end directly at the person. Take turns so you can hear how well the sound travels.

In open air, sound waves spread out and travel in all directions from the source (Fig. 42-5). When you use a megaphone, however, the energy of the sound waves is concentrated in one direction. This allows the sound to travel much further.

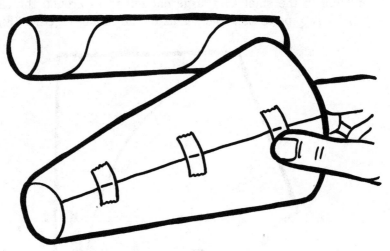

Fig. 42-2. Use tape to hold it together.

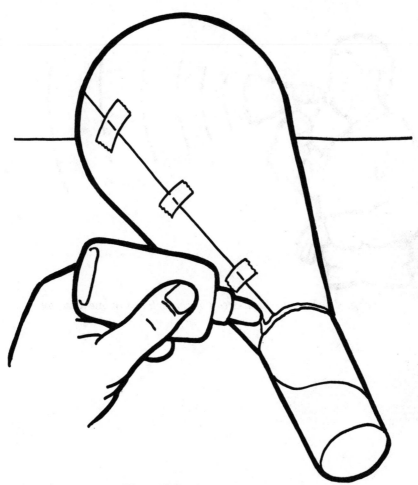

Fig. 42-3. *Glue the tube in place.*

Fig. 42-4. *Sound waves can be concentrated in one direction.*

Fig. 42-5. Sound waves spread out in open air.

Experiment 43

How to Make a Tin Can Telephone

Begin by waxing the string. Run the wax, back and forth, over the string several times (Fig. 43-1). Using the hammer and nail, make a small hole in the center of the bottom of each can (Fig. 43-2). Now thread one end of the string through the hole in one of the cans. Push

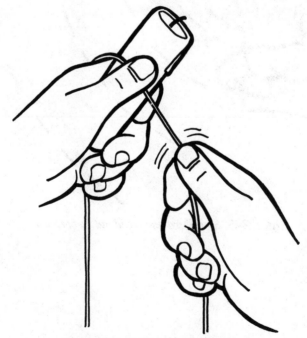

Fig. 43-1. Apply wax to the string.

the string through from the bottom then pull it out the opening at the top (Fig. 43-3). Thread the string through a button and tie a knot (Fig. 43-4). This is to keep the string from being pulled back through the hole. Repeat the steps with the other can at the other end of the string. Ask someone to hold one of the cans while you stretch the string out taut, holding the other can (Fig. 43-5). Be sure the string doesn't touch anything but the cans.

This experiment works best outside and away from any walls that might reflect sound. Ask the other person to speak into the can they're holding while you listen in yours. You will have to take turns talking and listening.

When you talk into the cans, you start the air inside vibrating. This causes the can to vibrate which in turn, makes the string vibrate. The string makes the other can vibrate and that allows the other person to hear what you say.

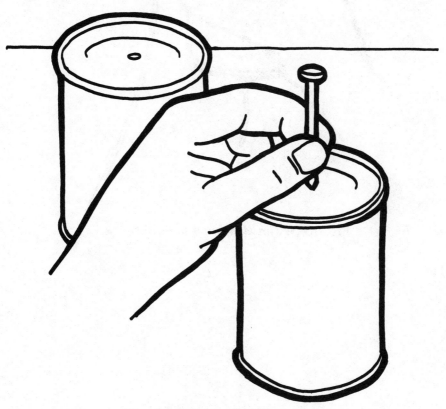

Fig. 43-2. Make a hole in each can.

***Fig. 43-3.** Thread the string through the hole.*

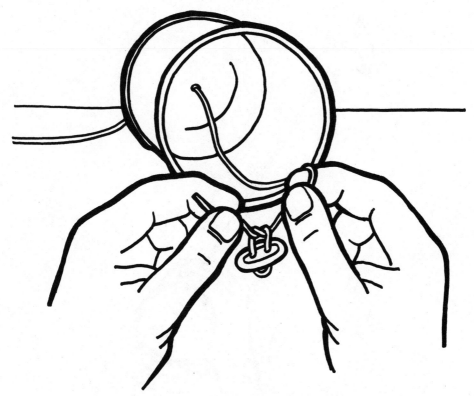

Fig. 43-4. *Tie a button to the string.*

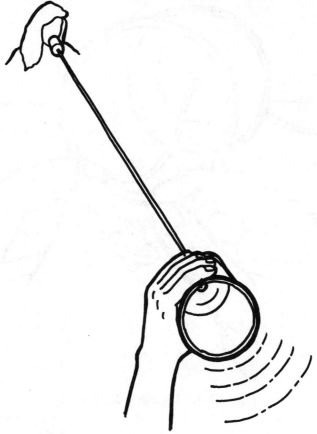

Fig. 43-5. *The stretched string will carry sound.*

Experiment 44

How to Make a Pin Piano

Materials

- ☐ 9 straight pins
- ☐ piece of soft wood (about 3" × 6", 1" thick)
- ☐ wooden pencil with eraser
- ☐ large baking pan
- ☐ small hammer
- ☐ pliers (with wire cutters)

Using the pliers, grasp one of the pins firmly near the sharp end and press it into the board. Push it in just far enough so that it is held secure. Place this first pin in the middle and near one end of the board as shown in Fig. 44-1. The pin should stick straight up. Press the next pin in place about a half inch down the board from the first. Drive this pin a little deeper. Repeat the steps until you have eight pins sticking up in a row. Each pin should be a little shorter than the one before it (see Fig. 44-2). You might have to use the hammer to tap some of them in. You might also have to cut one or two off to make them short enough. When you cut a pin, use the pliers and hold the pin inside a waste basket so that the unused end will be safely discarded (Fig. 44-3). Cut the head off the last pin, and using the pliers, press the large end straight into the top of the eraser (Fig. 44-4). This is what you'll use to stroke the pins.

Begin testing with the tallest pin; stroke it. This will be the lowest note. Continue with each pin, tapping them in or pulling them out a little until you have them tuned. Now stroke the full length of the pins and notice the sound (Fig. 44-5). It will be musical but not very loud. Put the baking pan upside down on a table and place the board on the pan. Now try it again (Fig. 44-6). It will be much louder.

The taller pins made the lower sounds because they were longer and vibrated at a slower speed than the shorter ones. The vibrations travelled through the board to the pan. The pan amplified the vibrations and made the sound louder.

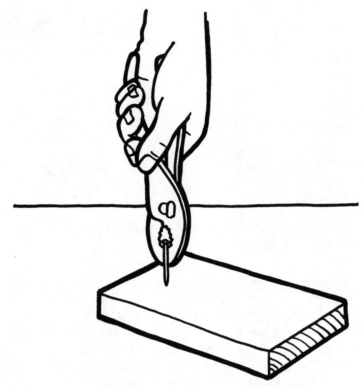

Fig. 44-1. *Press the pins into the board.*

Fig. 44-2. *Some pins might have to be tapped in with a hammer.*

Fig. 44-3. *Carefully cut the head from one of the pins over a waste basket.*

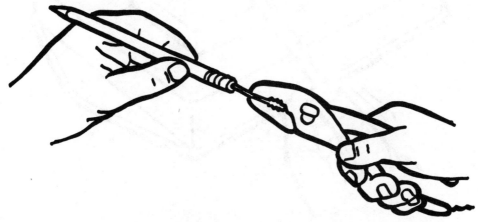

Fig. 44-4. *Press the big end into the eraser.*

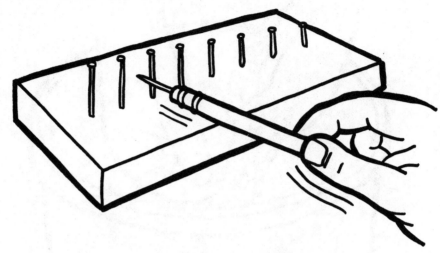

Fig. 44-5. *Stroke the pins to make musical sounds.*

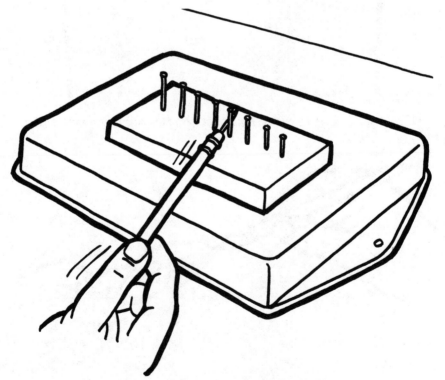

Fig. 44-6. *The pan will amplify the sound.*

Experiment 45

Materials

- [ ] board (about 2 feet long)
- [ ] 2 pencils
- [ ] strong thread (about 3 feet long)
- [ ] nail and hammer
- [ ] weight (bag of marbles or fishing sinkers)

How Notes Change on a Guitar

Hammer the nail a little way into the board near one end as shown in Fig. 45-1. Tie one end of the thread to the nail at a point next to the board. Tie the other end of the thread to the weight. Place the board on a table. Lay the pencils across the board about 12 inches apart.

Fig. 45-1. Drive the nail into the board.

Place the thread over both pencils and over the end of the board. Let the weight hang over the edge of the table (Fig. 45-2). The weight will keep the thread taut. Pluck the thread and notice the sound. Move the pencils a little closer together and pluck the thread again (Fig. 45-3). The note will be higher. Pluck the thread gently then harder. The sound will be louder but the pitch will be the same. The shorter the space between the pencils, the higher the pitch will be. This is because the shorter string will vibrate faster than a longer one. The faster the vibration, the higher the pitch. Figure 45-4 is a good illustration of this.

Fig. 45-2. *Stretch the thread over the pencils.*

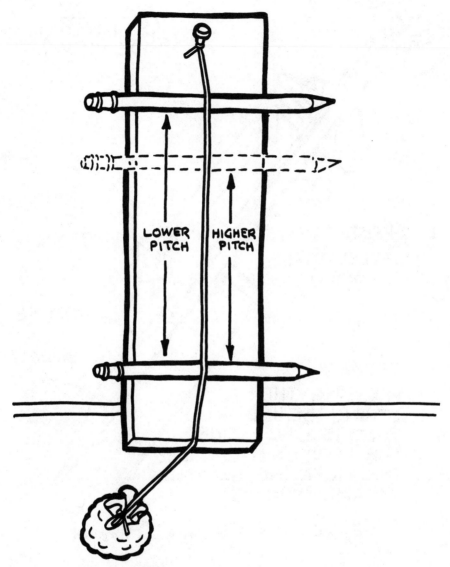

LOWER
PITCH

HIGHER
PITCH

Fig. 45-3. *The pitch can be changed when the thread is plucked.*

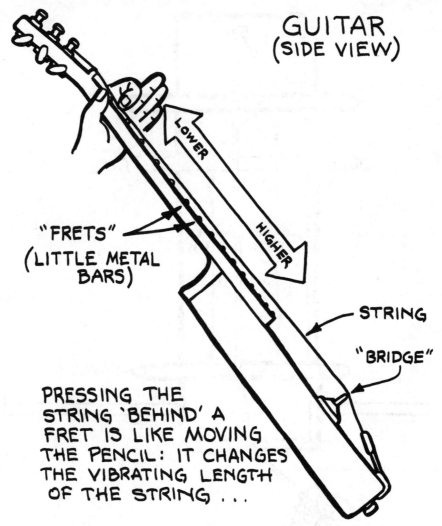

GUITAR
(SIDE VIEW)

LOWER

HIGHER

"FRETS"
(LITTLE METAL
BARS)

STRING

"BRIDGE"

PRESSING THE
STRING 'BEHIND' A
FRET IS LIKE MOVING
THE PENCIL: IT CHANGES
THE VIBRATING LENGTH
OF THE STRING . . .

Fig. 45-4. This is how notes are changed on a guitar.

Experiment 46

Materials

- ☐ **2 people**
- ☐ **loud, ticking clock**
- ☐ **tape measure**
- ☐ **day with a small breeze**

How Moving Air Affects Sound Waves

Ask someone to hold the clock, and see how far away you can be and still hear it. Measure this distance (Fig. 46-1). Now, go outside and notice which way the breeze is blowing. Slowly move away from the

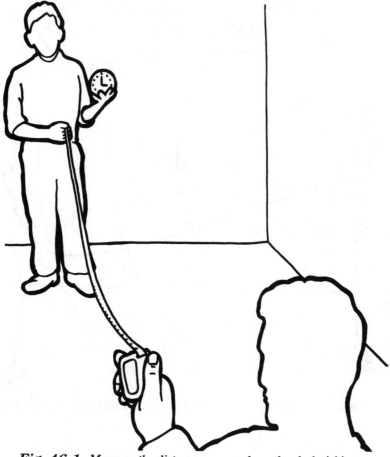

Fig. 46-1. Measure the distance you can hear the clock ticking.

person holding the clock. Move with the wind, in the direction that the breeze is blowing. Listen to the clock and stop when you can barely hear the ticking. Measure this distance (Fig. 46-2). Now, return to the clock and move into the wind, in the direction that the breeze is coming from (Fig. 46-3). Stop when you can barely hear the clock. Measure this distance and compare the other measurements. Take turns and see if the other person gets similar results.

The sound waves of the ticking clock were travelling in air, so the sound of the ticking can be heard at a greater distance when the sound was travelling with the air than against it.

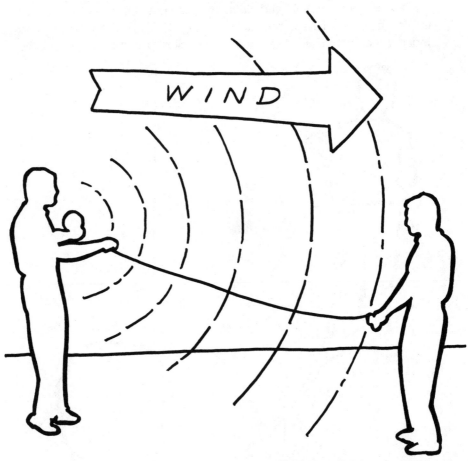

Fig. 46-2. Measure the distance you can hear with the wind in your face.

Fig. 46-3. Measure the distance with the wind at your back, then compare the distances.

Experiment 47

Materials

- ☐ 2 people
- ☐ cardboard tube from paper towels
- ☐ 2 spoons
- ☐ chair

Our Brain Can Measure the Difference in the Speed of Sound

Fig. 47-1. *Tap the spoons together on one side of their head.*

Ask someone to sit in the chair while you stand behind them. Ask them to raise their left hand when they hear a sound coming from their left side, the right hand when the sound comes from their right, and both hands when the sound comes from directly behind their head. Begin testing by tapping the spoons together once about a foot behind, and to one side of their head (Fig. 47-1). Next, tap the spoons together on the other side of their head, then straight behind their head (Fig. 47-2). Each time they will raise the correct hand and both hands when the sound was directly behind them. Now, ask them to hold one end of the tube against their ear while the other end sticks straight out to the side (Fig. 47-3).

Fig. 47-2. *Tap the spoons together directly behind their head.*

Repeat the steps and you will see that they think the sound came from behind their head when actually it came from behind the tube. This is because the brain can measure the difference between the time it takes the sound waves to reach one ear and the time it takes for the waves to reach the other ear. In the first part of the experiment, the brain was able to calculate the distance between the two ears. In the second part, the brain knew the distance between the open end of the tube and the ear on the opposite side of the head. Take turns and see if you hear the sounds the same way.

Fig. 47-3. *Notice the difference when the tube is used.*

Experiment 48

How a Phonograph Record Makes Sounds

Materials

☐ record player
☐ old record (one you can destroy)
☐ straight pin or needle
☐ sheet of paper
☐ magnifying glass
☐ transparent tape

Hold the record under a light and look at the surface with the magnifying glass. You will be able to see tiny grooves (Fig. 48-1). Origi-

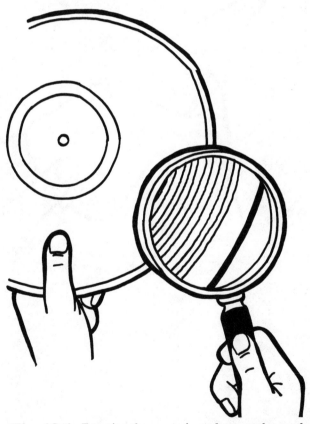

Fig. 48-1. Examine the groves in a phonograph record.

nally, the disk was smooth. The grooves were put in by a cutting needle that vibrated with the waves of the sound that was being recorded. Place the record on the player and start it to spin. Make a cone out of the sheet of paper using the tape to hold it together (Fig. 48-2). Fold the small end over and thread the pin through the folded part (Fig. 48-3). Now, gently lower the sharp end of the pin into the groove (Fig. 48-4). You will hear the sound that was recorded. It will not be very clear because the pin and cone amplifier are not too efficient.

The pin vibrated in the groove at the same rate as the sound that was recorded. The cone amplified the sound so you could hear it.

Fig. 48-2. Make a paper cone.

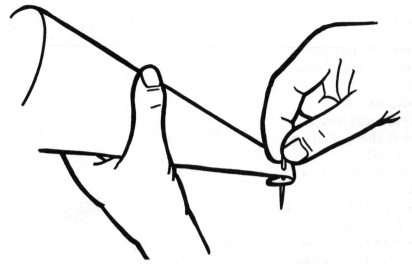

Fig. 48-3. *Press a pin through the end of the cone.*

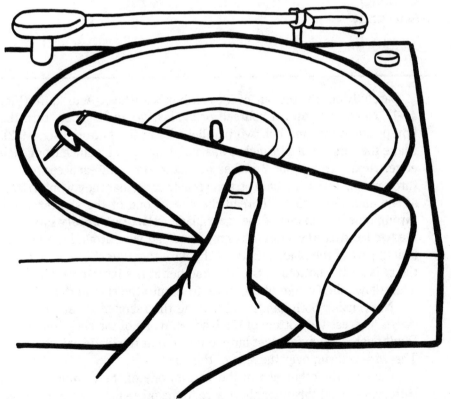

Fig. 48-4. *Lower the pin into the groove.*

Experiment 49

How a Telephone Works

Materials

- [ ] empty, round salt box
- [ ] 2, single-edge razor blades
- [ ] pencil lead from mechanical pencil or pencil sharpened on both ends
- [ ] 9 volt battery (from transistor radio)
- [ ] old telephone receiver or speaker from a radio
- [ ] 3 lengths of copper wire (1 about 6 feet long and 2 about 3 feet long)
- [ ] X-Acto knife

Carefully cut the top out of the salt box with the X-Acto knife (Fig. 49-1). Never cut toward yourself or against yourself. Then, turn the box upside down and cut two parallel slits in the bottom (Fig. 49-2). Make the slits about 1½ inches apart and an equal distance from each edge. Next, strip about 2 inches of insulation from each end of the three wires. Twist the bare strands together so that they won't frizzle at the ends (Fig. 49-3). Thread the end of one of the shorter wires through the hole in one of the razor blades. (**Be extremely careful. Razor blades are very sharp.**) Bend the wire around the bottom (thick) part of the blade and twist the wire together (Fig. 49-4). Place the twist at the bottom of the hole and not at the bottom of the blade. This allows the bottom of the blade to fit into the slits in the box.

Next, using both hands and holding the razor blade at each end, *carefully* press the bottom of the blade into one of the slits (Fig. 49-5). Don't push it in too far. Just far enough so that the blade will stand up. The wire will run over the side of the box.

Connect the other end of the wire to one of the terminals of the battery. Connect the other short wire to the other battery terminal and one of the terminals on the speaker. Connect one end of the longer wire to the other terminal of the speaker (Fig. 49-6). Now you need to connect the other end of the wire to the other razor blade the same way the first blade was connected.

Insert the bottom of this blade in the remaining slit. Place the pencil lead across the top of the two blades. This makes the final electrical connection. Place your ear close to the speaker and gently touch the box with your fingernail (Fig. 49-7). You will hear a noise something like static on a radio.

When you touched the box with your finger, it caused the box to vibrate. This made the razor blades vibrate. When the sharp edges of the blades vibrated, they moved rapidly against the pencil lead. This caused the electrical current to flow in a pattern, or frequency, like that of the vibrations made by the razor blades. When this pulsating current reaches the speaker, it travels to an electromagnet that is attached to the fiber cone of the speaker. The current makes the coil of the electromagnet move in and out and this causes the cone to vibrate, producing the same sound that was sent from the box.

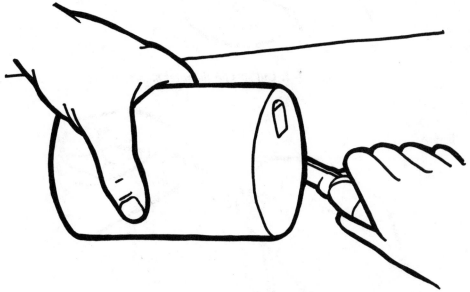

Fig. 49-1. *Cut the top out of the box.*

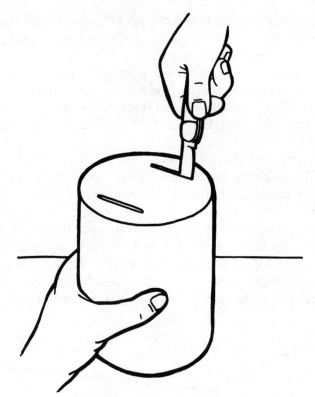

Fig. 49-2. *Cut slits for the razor blades.*

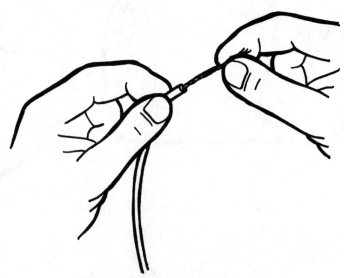

Fig. 49-3. *Twist the strands together.*

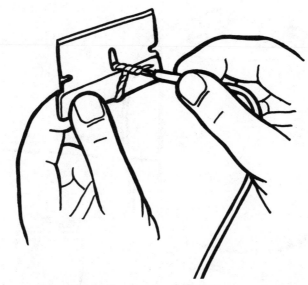

Fig. 49-4. *Connect the wire to the razor blade.*

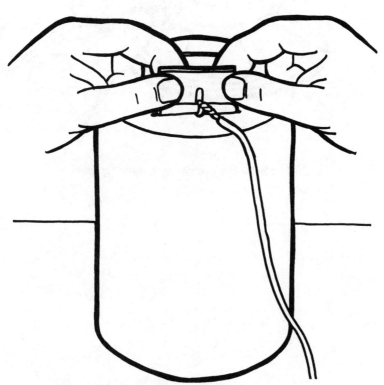

Fig. 49-5. *Carefully press the blade into the slit.*

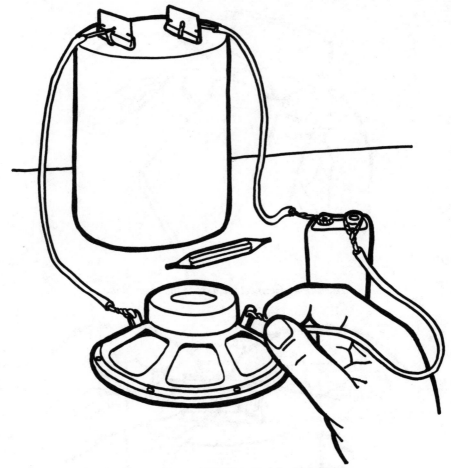

Fig. 49-6. *Connect the wires to the speaker.*

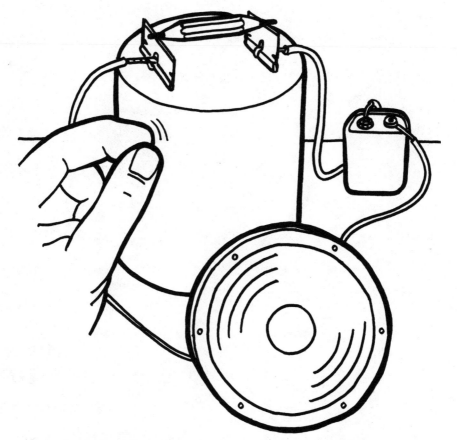

Fig. 49-7. *Place the lead across the blades and touch the box.*

PART II

SCIENCE FAIR
PROJECTS

Taking part in a science fair can be an exciting and rewarding experience. To increase your chances of having a successful project, you should organize your project into several basic steps:

1. Choosing a topic.
2. Forming a hypothesis. A hypothesis is just your guess of what the results of the experiment will be.
3. Doing the experiment.
4. Displaying the results and conclusions of your experiment.

Probably the most difficult part of doing a science fair project is choosing a subject. Spend a lot of time deciding on the subject and what you want the experiment to accomplish. This is very important, because if you hastily choose a subject that later turns out to be too complicated or the materials are not available, you'll quickly lose interest in the project.

You will also want to choose a project that is within your abilities and that interests you. This will help to keep you enthused if you run into problems. Also, choose a project that has materials that are easy to obtain. Keep in mind that an important part of a science fair project is how well you use your imagination. It is amazing how exotic a project can be and still be made up of basic materials. A simple, well demonstrated experiment can be much more important than a complicated experiment that is poorly done.

Once you have decided on a subject, you should choose a specific question to the answered or a particular problem to solve. Don't generalize. For example, you might hypothesize that airwaves travel faster than sound waves. You could use the experiment on how to make an air shock wave to demonstrate the comparison between airwaves and sound waves. Or you might set up a glass tank with a light under it. You could pour in a little water, drop a drop of water in one end, and produce shadow wave patterns on the ceiling.

You might decide to test how sound travels through different materials by setting up a long, wooden table and a tank of water to demonstrate how the sound travels through different materials.

The experiment where you rub your finger around the rim of a glass could be used to show how vibrations produce sound. This could be expanded to include the experiment about the telephone transmitter that uses the pencil lead and the two razor blades. This time, you could use an old telephone receiver (Fig. 1) and place a clock inside the box. People attending the fair could stop and listen to the ticking. Instead of a clock, you could use a small transistor radio turned very low and produce music in the receiver.

You should probably make a report on your experiment that explains what you wanted to prove or that simply answers a question you wanted answered. You might even want to add charts or graphs of your data. Charts and graphs can be very helpful in explaining experiments. The report should describe your hypothesis, how the experiment was done, and your results and conclusions. Therefore, be sure you write things down as you do your experiment. Your observations of time, quantities, distances, test materials, etc., will make up the data you need to do a report.

Once you have decided on a subject and formed a hypothesis, you need to plan on how you'll want to display your experiment. You might want to start saving normal, home throw-away items such as cardboard tubes from paper towels, coffee cans, glass or plastic bottles, and wooden spools from thread.

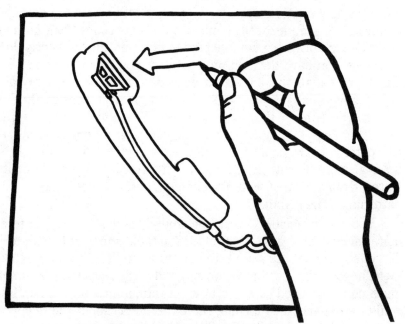

Fig. 1. *Use an old telephone receiver.*

Usually, experiments are displayed using panels that can be built from wood or cardboard that is divided into three sections. The ends are bent slightly forward to make the panel self-supporting.

The panels contain information about your experiment. For example, if you choose the telephone experiment, the left part of the panel could show some early history about communication and your hypothesis. The center of the panel could show how your experiment is constructed and the right part of the panel might show proof of how sound vibrations are converted into electrical signals and then back into sound (Fig. 2), possibly using graphs and

Fig. 2. *Your display should explain your project clearly.*

charts. Use all of your data and any models that you built. What your model will look like will largely depend on how creative you can be.

Scientists and other professionals have been studying sound for hundreds of years, but progress has made giant steps in recent years, and new discoveries are now made almost daily. Acoustics is an exciting science, expanding in all directions, including manufacturing products, weather forecasting, and medicine. By using your imagination, you can turn the simplest of experiments into one that will be very interesting.

Index